About Her

-Lalmalsawm Guite

First published in 2025

Printed by Amazon Kindle Direct Publishing

Preface

About Her is more than a book, it's a quiet conversation with the past.

It's for the girl who never knew how deeply she was loved.
And for the ones who loved without answers, who stayed longer in their thoughts than they did in someone's life.

These pages are filled with pieces of what was felt but never said heartbreaks, hopes, almost and healing.

If you've ever carried someone in silence, this book is for you.

-Lalmalsawm Guite

INTRODUCTION

About Her

She wasn't just one girl.
She was every girl we ever loved and maybe never got to love fully.
She was the first heartbreak.
The almost.
The what if.
The one who stayed too long, or the one who left too soon.

This is not just *my* story.
It's *ours.*
It's *yours* even if you've never said her name out loud.
Even if you've buried her deep in the corners of memory,
you'll find her here.

She might be the girl whose laugh you still hear in crowded rooms.
The girl you tried to forget, but never really could.
The one you let go of or the one who let go of you.

This book is a collection of moments,
of truths too soft to shout,
of feelings too loud to ignore.

For every guy who's ever waited for a text that never came.
For every girl who's ever wondered if she was ever *really* seen.
For anyone who's ever held love in their hands and then watched it slip away.

She lives in these pages.
In the pauses.
In the unwritten lines between chapters.
In the songs we avoid because they still feel like her.

This isn't a happy story.
This isn't a sad one either.
It's a real one.

This book is *About Her*
but somehow, it's also about *you.*

Part I: Falling for Her

Memory I: The Way She Laughed

Memory II: The First Time I Saw Her

Memory III: When She Didn't Know I Was Watching

Memory IV: Her Eyes Were My Home

Memory V: She Was Chaos in a Beautiful Dress

Memory VI: The Girl Who Made Time Feel Too Fast

Memory VII: I Remember Her in Every Song

Memory VIII: When She Said My Name

Memory IX: The Way She Touched My Soul

Memory X: She Was Magic, Not Mine

Part II: In Love with Her

Letter I: She Taught Me How to Feel

Letter II: About Her and the Little Things

Letter III: The Way She Held My Hand

Letter IV: The Way She Looked at Me

Letter V: The Way She Smiled when She said my Name

Letter VI: The Night Everything felt like Forever

Letter VII: The Mornings with Her

Letter VIII: Her Favorite Color Became Mine

Letter IX: When She Looked at Me Like I Was Enough

Letter X: The Smile I Wanted to Protect

Part III: Losing Her

Echo I: The Day She Left

Echo II: The Silence That Followed

Echo III: I Miss Her in Crowds

Echo IV: Her Goodbye Broke Me Quietly

Echo V: The Things I Never Said

Echo VI: About Her and the Distance

Echo VII: She Forgot Me Slowly

Echo VIII: When Love Wasn't Enough

Echo IX: I Waited, She Didn't Come Back

Echo X: I Still Write Her Name Sometimes

Part IV: Living Without Her

Reflection I: If She's Reading This...

Reflection II: About Her and the Ghost She Left

Reflection III: Every Girl After Her

Reflection IV: When I Saw Her Again

Reflection V: The Dreams Where She Returns

Reflection VI: Healing Is Remembering Without Crying

Reflection VII: She Was a Lesson, Not a Loss

Reflection VIII: I Hope She's Loved Now

Reflection IX: What I'd Say If I Could

Reflection X: About Her, Always

PART I: FALLING FOR HER

"Sometimes, we fall in love by accident.
But the truth is
we were already falling the moment we noticed her."

Memory I: The Way She Laughed

There are memories that don't fade
not because they were the loudest,
but because they made everything else go quiet.

Hers was the kind of laugh
that didn't just echo in rooms.
It echoed in people.

It wasn't the kind of laugh you'd hear in a movie scene,
graceful and neatly timed.
It was real.
Honest.
The kind that spilled out suddenly,
like a child running into the rain.
It came with no warning,
no apology,
and no care for how the world saw her in that moment.

She laughed like she forgot the world was watching.
And in those seconds,
so did I.

When she laughed, her whole face changed.
Her eyes squinted with joy,
her nose crinkled just a bit,
and sometimesif the joke was stupid enough,
or the timing just right
she'd snort.
She'd turn pink, embarrassed,
and then cover her mouth and say,
"Don't ever tell anyone I do that."

But I'm telling you now.

Because I remember.
Because I still hear it in quiet places
in the background of a long drive,
in the silence before I fall asleep.
That laugh.
Still hers.
Still mine, in a way.

She wasn't always like that.
Most days she carried herself like a whisper
careful, folded in,
as if trying not to take up too much space.
But when she laughed,
something broke free.
Something *true.*

You could see it
the armor slipping off,
the posture softening,
the girl who tried so hard to hold herself together
finally letting herself fall apart
in the best way.

And I loved her most then.

Not when she was polished or prepared,
but when she forgot to be.
When she stopped trying to look composed,
and just *was.*

You learn a lot about people by how they laugh.
Some laugh like they're asking for permission.
She laughed like she was made of stars
and didn't need permission from anyone.

Once, I said something stupid
probably by accident
and she burst.
Threw her head back,
hit the table with her hand,
snorted mid-laugh,
and then immediately covered her face,
mumbling something like,
"I hate you" through a grin.

God, I wish I could live in that moment.
Just one more time.

You don't think a laugh can change your life.
But then someone laughs like that near you,
because of you,
with you
and you realize,
that sound is what love might look like
if you could hear it.

It wasn't just a laugh.
It was a confession.
A key turned quietly in the lock.
A tiny rebellion against everything that tried to keep her guarded.

And the world
my world
has been quieter ever since she stopped laughing near me.

But if you listen closely,
if you really try…
You might still hear it.

Still ringing.
Still warm.
Still hers.

Memory II: The First Time I Saw Her

The first time I saw her,
she didn't see me.

She walked into the room like the room had been waiting.
Not because she tried
but because the space seemed to breathe her in.
The light shifted.
The air stilled.
And time… blinked.

Not a dramatic halt.
More like the hush between heartbeats.
The way a leaf stops trembling when the wind dies.

I can't remember what she wore.
But I remember the atmosphere
soft and golden, like the kind of light that happens just before a beautiful secret is told.
I remember the way the sun found her hair,
how it clung to each strand like it, too, wanted to stay longer.

Her voice rose
not loudly,
but like music you hear before you even realize you're listening.
It wasn't a voice that demanded.
It invited.
It lingered.

She didn't smile at me.
Didn't look my way.
But something in me leaned forward.
A pause beneath the ribs.

A whisper without words:
"There she is."

It wasn't love.
Not yet.
It was quieter than that.
Like the hush before dawn.
A gentle, magnetic wondering.
A soft gravitational pull from something I hadn't yet begun to understand.

She laughed at someone else's joke,
and I found myself memorizing the sound.
Pretending not to notice.
But already addicted.

And I remember asking myselfwhy her?
There were other people, other faces,
but none of them made time slow.
None of them rearranged the air.

She wasn't trying to be noticed.
She wasn't polished or filtered.
She was simply…
her.
Unrehearsed.
Unapologetically human.
Like a poem that forgot it was being read aloud.

The first time I saw her, I didn't know she'd become a story I'd write again and again in my head.
I didn't know that moment would become a landmark in my memory.
That it would have its own weight. Its own echo.

But I think my heart knew.
Before I did.

Before anything else.
Before even the second breath.

Because that's how it starts sometimes
not with fireworks,
not with lightning,
but with a quiet second…
and someone who makes you feel like the wait is over.

Memory III: When She Didn't Know I Was Watching

There were moments
the kind the world doesn't notice
when she was just herself.
No performance. No pretending.
Moments when she thought no one was looking.

And in those quiet seconds,
she became something more than beautiful
she became *real.*

She'd sit with one leg folded beneath her,
hair cascading in soft waves,
face gentle and unguarded,
eyes tracing thoughts only she knew.

She'd bite her lip when lost in wonder.
Tap rhythms on the table when the world moved too slow.
Mutter secrets to herself under her breath
not stories, but half-formed thoughts,
like prayers spoken only to silence.

And sometimes,
she would laugh
not the laugh she gave to crowds,
not the bright one that lit rooms,
but the quiet one,
the fragile, forgotten laugh
that belonged only to her.

I watched her once
sitting by the window,

where sunlight traced soft golden lines across her face.
A book in her lap, pages barely turned.
She wasn't reading.
She was somewhere else.
Maybe in a memory.
Maybe in a place I couldn't follow.
Maybe with someone who wasn't me.

She brushed her hair behind her ear without knowing.
Sipped tea that had gone cold.
Looked at the empty air
like it held answers she couldn't ask out loud.

And I just sat there
breathless,
still,
memorizing the poetry of her simply being.

There's something sacred
about seeing someone
when they don't know they're being seen.
That's when you witness their truth
unpolished,
unmasked,
untouched by expectation.

When she didn't know I was watching,
she was raw and infinite.
Not filtered for affection,
not crafted for attention
just *her*.

And maybe that's when I loved her most.
Not for the light she shared with the world,
but for the shadows she kept for herself.

For the version the world didn't earn
but I got to see.

By accident.
By chance.
By grace.

Memory IV: Her Eyes Were My Home

There was something about her eyes
not just their shape or shade,
but the way they knew me
before I ever spoke.

They weren't perfect.
No, they carried shadows,
the kind only sorrow could paint.
Like they'd seen wars no one else noticed,
like they'd stayed open through nights
that should've broken her.

But even in their weariness,
they held a quiet kind of strength
like a lighthouse that keeps shining
even after the ship has sunk.

When she looked at me
truly looked
the world hushed.
I didn't have to try.
Didn't have to explain.
Didn't have to hide.
Her gaze wrapped around my flaws
like it had been made
to hold even the messiest parts of me.

They said,
"You're safe."
"You're seen."
"You're still worth loving."

Those eyes held both winter and wildfire.
They could freeze you with the truth
or melt you with a glance.
They weren't just eyes
they were a sanctuary.
A soft place to land
when the world had grown too loud.

Sometimes, she looked at the world
like it had betrayed her.
Other times,
like she still believed it could change.
And I loved both versions.
Because both were her.
Because both made me want to protect her,
even from herself.

I remember one night
nothing but silence between us,
the kind that said everything
without asking for anything.
She looked at me,
and in that one second,
I didn't need a future,
or a forever,
or even a kiss.
I just needed that moment
those eyes,
that stillness,
the fragile miracle of being seen.

Her eyes became my home.
Not because they made life easier,
but because they made it make sense.

Even when I didn't know who I was,
even when the world told me I was too broken
those eyes whispered,
"Come in anyway."

And though time moved forward
though people left,
though she left
I still search for them.

In crowds.
In memories.
In dreams I wake up aching from.

But nothing else feels like home,
once you've belonged to someone's eyes
and lost them.

Memory V: She Was Chaos in a Beautiful Dress

She wasn't calm.
She wasn't the quiet kind of girl who sat still and smiled politely,
the type who crossed her legs neatly and waited to be invited.
No
She entered every room like the door owed her something.
Like life owed her a stage and she was tired of asking for it.

She was a storm wrapped in silk,
a wildfire painted in lipstick,
a thunderclap hiding inside a smile that could disarm your logic.
She was laughter at a funeral,
tears during a comedy,
and the loudest silence you've ever heard in your life.

She didn't walk
she swayed like music nobody else could hear.
And when she laughed,
God, when she laughed
it was like the sky cracked open and begged for more of her sound.

She danced like nobody was watching
even when everyone was.
And she argued like truth itself depended on her voice.
Not to win
but because she couldn't stomach the idea of staying silent
when something needed to be said.
Even if it made her the villain in someone else's story.

Her thoughts were like fireworks
never on schedule,
always unexpected,
and blindingly beautiful.

She'd interrupt herself mid-sentence,
apologize,
laugh,
and then circle back with something even more brilliant
than what she started with.

She was late to everything
but when she arrived,
time stopped making sense.
You'd forget the wait,
the reason,
the world
because suddenly, she was the only thing worth noticing.

She tripped over her own feet,
spilled coffee on her favorite books,
and lost her phone at least twice a week.
She once wore mismatched shoes to a wedding and called it "intentional chaos."
And somehow,
every accident became part of her legend.

People said she was "too much."
Too loud.
Too emotional.
Too intense.
But that's because they were too little
too fragile to carry a soul like hers.
They didn't see the poetry in her chaos,
only the volume.
But I did.

I saw how she cried in elevators and made friends in grocery stores.
I saw how she stayed up all night writing letters she'd never send
and dancing with songs only she remembered.

I saw her hold broken people with hands still bleeding from her own battles.

She was a paradox
soft eyes and sharp tongue,
tender heart and untamed spirit.
She could light up a room
or burn it down
and you'd still thank her for either.

She wasn't born to be understood.
She was born to be felt.
To be experienced like art
not explained like logic.

And I
I was just a soul lucky enough to orbit her world for a while.
To witness her fire up close.
To be burned, yes,
but also awakened.

Because some people are calm seas.
But she?
She was the storm that reminded you what it felt like to be alive.

She was chaos.
Unapologetic, unstoppable, unforgettable chaos...
in a beautiful dress.

And if I could do it all over again,
I wouldn't try to tame her.
I wouldn't try to change her.
I'd simply lace my fingers through hers
and whisper:

"Burn, baby, burn. I'm not afraid of the fire."

Memory IV: The Girl Who Made Time Feel Too Fast

Some people walk into your life and everything slows down.
Their presence stretches out the hours, lingers in the air like a sigh that never finishes.
You watch the clock tick with them
a slow, aching rhythm.
But not her.
She was the opposite of slow.

She made time run.

With her, every second slipped through my fingers like water.
We'd sit down for "just a minute,"
but the minute became an hour,
and the hour became a memory,
and that memory now feels like it's chasing me
always out of reach.

She didn't just *talk* fast.
She *lived* fast.
Not recklessly
but fully.
Like she was in on a secret the rest of us hadn't figured out yet.
Like life was a song she didn't want to pause,
a beat she couldn't stop dancing to.

And me?
I was just trying to keep up.
Trying to hold on to every word she said,
every look she gave,
every little moment she shared like it was a gift,
wrapped in laughter and lit by the way her eyes flickered when she got excited.

She'd tell stories that never had endings,
thoughts that spilled into other thoughts
chaotic, beautiful, alive.
Sometimes I didn't understand the point.
Sometimes there was no point.
And yet, I listened.
Because when she spoke,
the world went quiet.
Even time seemed to lean in.

I never looked at my phone.
Never wondered what came next.
Because I knewwhatever came next,
I'd wish it wasn't coming so soon.

We always think we'll have more time.
We think we'll find another moment to say what matters.
Another day to laugh.
Another night to remember.
But with her, time was greedy.
It stole her away piece by piece
even while she was still right in front of me.

And now?
Now the hours stretch.
Now the mornings feel longer, the nights heavier.
The silence she used to fill feels louder than any noise I've known.
I replay those moments in my mind
her laugh,
her stories,
her interruptions,
the way she'd get distracted mid-thought and forget what she was saying
and I remember how fast it all went.

How little I said.
How much I felt.
And how badly I wanted it to last just a little longer.

But you can't hold time.
And you can't hold people like her.
They were never meant to stay still.

She was the girl who made time feel too fast.
And now she's the memory that makes time feel too slow.

But I'd still do it all over again.
I'd race through those hours again,
lose track of the days again,
just to feel what I felt when she looked at me
like I was the moment she didn't want to miss.

Maybe she never knew.
Maybe I never told her.
But she changed the way I counted time
not in hours,
not in days,
but in how deeply a soul could make you feel
within the space of a single afternoon.

And maybe that's what love is
not forever.
Not always.
But the way someone makes one fleeting moment
feel like the best part of your entire life.

Memory VII: I Remember Her in Every Song

It's strange how music does that
brings her back without warning.
Not like a memory,
but like a presence.
Soft. Heavy. Inevitable.

Sometimes it's a song we both loved
the one we played on repeat during late-night calls,
our voices tangled with the static,
talking about everything and nothing.
Sometimes, it's a song she never even knew,
but somehow,
the lyrics sound like her.

There's a melody for her laughter.
A bassline for the weight of her silence.
A verse for the way she walked away
slow, certain, without turning back.

I'll be standing in line,
or driving,
or sitting still in a room that suddenly doesn't feel so empty
and there she is.
In a chord.
In a bridge.
In a line that splits me open.

Funny, how a voice from a speaker
can feel closer than a touch.
Familiar, like breath on skin I haven't felt in years.

And I don't skip them anymore.
Even when it hurts.
Even when I have to close my eyes
and let the pain rise like smoke in my throat.

Because some songs aren't just music.
They're places.
Road trips.
Kitchens full of laughter.
Stars overhead on nights that felt infinite.

The songs never ask if I'm ready.
They just arrive.
And so does she
with every note,
every lyric she once quoted,
every beat she once danced to barefoot in my kitchen.

She used to close her eyes and say,
"God, this song is so me."

Now?
They're all so *her*.
Every last one.

I remember her in every song
not because I want to,
but because music never forgets
what the heart refuses to bury.

She became my favorite playlist
and the hardest one to listen to.

Memory VIII: When She Said My Name

There was a way she said my name
that no one else could ever echo.
Not in sound
but in *weight.*
It wasn't just pronunciation.
It was intention.
It was presence.
It was *hers.*

She didn't say it often.
She didn't need to.
But when she did
when she really meant it
the noise of the world dimmed,
and everything softened.

She'd say it while laughing,
like I was part of a secret
she'd never share with anyone else.
She'd say it when she was annoyed,
drawing it out just long enough
to make me grin.

She whispered it on quiet nights
when the space between us spoke louder than words.
And once
just once
she said it like a promise.
Like a prayer.

Like my name was safe
in the only mouth that would ever hold it right.

I never told her
how much it meant.
How hearing it from her lips
made me feel seen
not just noticed,
but *known*.

In a world full of strangers
saying my name out of habit or need,
she spoke it like she chose me.
Like she *meant* me.
Like she *saw* me.

Because she didn't just say my name.
She held it.
Carefully.
Deliberately.
Like it was fragile.
Like it was sacred.
Like it belonged somewhere
close to her heart.

Now, others say it.
They speak with kindness.
With care.
Sometimes even with love.
But none of them say it like she did.
None of them say it
like it *mattered*.

Memory IX: The Way She Touched My Soul

She never touched me like the world expects love to feel.

There were no grand gestures.
No candlelit confessions or movie-scene kisses.
No filtered photos to prove it happened.
She didn't need any of that.
Because she didn't touch my body
she touched something far deeper.
She touched my soul.

She reached the parts of me I thought were untouchable.
The places I had buried under years of silence.
The weight behind my "I'm fine."
The cracks behind my smile.
The echoes of things I never dared to say aloud.

And she didn't stumble upon them accidentally.
She *searched* for them.
Not to fix me.
Not to rescue me.
But to know me.
Fully.
Quietly.
Honestly.

She asked the questions others were too afraid to ask
not because she was curious,
but because she *cared.*
She listened like my pain was not a problem

but a language she was fluent in.
She held space for the parts of me I had always kept locked away
the little boy behind the man,
the trembling under my strength,
the softness I thought I had to sacrifice to survive.

And when she found those parts,
she didn't flinch.
She didn't leave.
She didn't try to polish them into something prettier.
She simply stayed.
With a stillness so rare,
it felt like grace.

She made me feel like my wounds weren't warnings.
Like my chaos wasn't a curse.
Like I could be held,
exactly as I was
broken, brave, and becoming.

And in her presence,
my shame learned how to speak.
My fears learned how to breathe.
My silence finally found a home.

She touched my soul
not with her hands,
but with her seeing.
With her patience.
With her unshakable belief
that even the messiest parts of me
deserved love.

And now, when I think of her,
I don't just miss her laugh,

or the curve of her smile,
or the way she said my name like a prayer.

I miss the version of me that existed in her eyes
the one who felt whole.
The one who didn't have to pretend.
The one who finally believed he was enough.

Because some people kiss your skin.
But she…
she kissed my being.
She loved me in the places no one else even looked.
And I don't know if anyone
will ever touch me like that again.

But God, I'm grateful
that someone ever did.

Memory X: She Was Magic, Not Mine

She wasn't loud magic
not the kind that turns heads
or demands applause.
She was quiet magic
the kind you feel
before you understand.
The kind that shifts your soul
slowly,
then all at once.

She had this way of being
of simply being
that made everything else
feel both too much
and not enough.

She didn't try to be different.
She just was.

The way she listened
like time paused
between your words.
The way she smiled
as if it came from somewhere
beyond this world.
The way she walked
as if she'd already
made peace
with every storm
she'd survived.

I used to think magic
meant tricks,
sparks,
illusions.

But then I watched her laugh
in the middle of pain.
Then I saw her choose kindness
for people who didn't deserve it.
Then I saw her believe
in others,
in me,
when I had nothing left to give.

She didn't cast spells.
She broke them.

She unraveled the ones
I'd wrapped around my soul
the lies I mistook for truth,
the fears I wore like skin,
the walls I thought were permanent.

She walked into my life
like light through a crack
not to blind me,
but to show me
what had always been
waiting in the dark.

And yes,
I wanted her to be mine.
To hold her.
To keep her.
To press her presence
into forever.

But people like her...
you don't keep them.

You witness them.
You honor them.
You thank God
for the rare miracle
of simply knowing them.

Because magic like hers
was never meant to be owned.
Only felt.
Only remembered.
Only missed.

And I miss her
not like a person,
but like a revelation.
A miracle
that only happens once
in a lifetime.

PART II: IN LOVE WITH HER

"Being in love wasn't loud.
It was in the way she reached for my hand without looking.
In the way silence felt full when she was beside me.
It was the comfort in her presence
like I'd finally found the place the world made sense."

Letter I: She Taught Me How to Feel

Before her,
I didn't know how to say what I was feeling.
Didn't know I was allowed
to feel this much.
I lived in my head
thoughts were easier than emotions,
logic safer than vulnerability.
Walls kept things neat.
But then she came
like sunlight spilling through a window
I didn't know existed.

She didn't talk about feelings.
She *lived* them.
Cried when movies hit too close.
Laughed too loud when life surprised her.
Held my hand like it was the most natural thing.
And when I spoke,
even in fragments,
she listened like each word
was a secret worth keeping.

She taught me that being strong
doesn't mean being numb.
That trembling can be part of courage.
That tears aren't surrender
they're truth spilling out of places
you've kept locked too long.
She made emotion sacred.

Something to be honored,
not hidden.

Love, she showed me,
wasn't always grand or loud.
Sometimes,
it was the silence that understood you.
The glance that said,
I'm here,
when you had no words left.
Sometimes,
it was letting your voice shake
and knowing someone was listening anyway.

She taught me that to open your heart
isn't to lose control
it's to trust
that someone will hold
what you're still learning
not to drop.

I didn't know how to feel.
Not really.
But she held a mirror to my heart,
and for the first time,
I didn't flinch.
Didn't look away.

And now
even when she's gone
I still feel.
And I still thank her
for giving me back
the parts of myself
I didn't know how to name.

Letter II: About Her and the Little Things

It wasn't the grand gestures.
Not the fireworks, the confessions under rain, or the sweeping cinematic moments.
No
It was the little things.

The details hidden in the quiet.
The things most people overlook.
But once I noticed them in her,
I could never unsee them.
I didn't want to.

It was the way she tucked her hair behind her ear when she was nervous like a silent signal only I could read.
The soft hum under her breath when she thought the world wasn't listening.
The habit of ordering extra fries
just in case I changed my mind.
(Even when I swore I wouldn't.
I always did.)

She said my name like it belonged somewhere safe.
Like it meant something.
She remembered everything
the throwaway sentences I thought she'd forget.
My favorite song.
That I liked my tea unsweetened.
That I sleep with the lights on.
She never forgot.

She loved rainy days,
but hated wet socks.
She'd carry an umbrella,
not for herself,
but for me.

She'd laugh at her own jokes before the punchline.
And whenever she saw a dog,
she lit up like a child seeing magic for the first time.

She always smelled like lavender,
and something warm,
something that felt like home.

Her texts weren't always timely
but they always came when I needed them most.
She believed in signs from the universe,
talked to the moon,
waved at babies in strollers.
Spoke kindly to waiters on days when she couldn't even be kind to herself.

She cried over sad books.
Got emotionally wrecked by fictional characters.
Had playlists for everything
walking, crying, dancing alone.

She made the world seem bearable.
Like maybe, just maybe,
it wasn't such a terrible place after all.

She'd say "I'm okay" when she wasn't
and I learned to hear the tremble in her voice.
Learned to stay.
To listen.
To see her, even when she was trying to disappear.

She didn't pull me in with force
just presence.
A gravity so gentle,
I barely noticed I'd fallen
until I realized I never wanted to get up.

She kept bandaids in her bag
for people she didn't even know.
Sent memes to lift the weight of my bad days.
Held my hand like it was a promise,
never rushed,
never loose,
always *there.*

She didn't need to care.
But she did.
Deeply.

She made space for me
not by clearing out her life,
but by expanding it,
like I had always belonged there.

She wasn't trying to be perfect.
She was just… real.
Unfiltered.
Unapologetically her.

And that
that made her unforgettable.

I used to think love had to be loud,
life-altering,
seismic.

But she taught me
Love is quiet.

It's in the everyday things.
The unspectacular moments that linger.

It's her stealing my hoodie and defending it like a courtroom lawyer.
It's her falling asleep mid-text but still typing,
"I'm listening."
It's her dancing barefoot in the kitchen,
spinning like the whole world belonged to her.

It's her.
It's always been her.

And all the little things she never knew she was doing
are now
the biggest parts of me.

Letter III: The Way She Held My Hand

It wasn't just fingers interlocked.
It wasn't just skin grazing skin.
When she held my hand, the world didn't just pause
it rearranged itself,
until nothing made sense except *us*.

She didn't hold my hand just to fill the space between us.
She held it when we crossed streets,
when we sat in silence,
when my thoughts ran too loud,
when my pride stood too tall.

She held it when I didn't even know I needed to be held.

The first time she reached for it,
she didn't ask.
She just *took* it
gently, reverently,
like she was learning how to hold something breakable
without letting it slip away.

And in that instant,
I knew
I was no longer walking through life alone.

She had her own language,
spoken entirely through touch:
A squeeze when she was thrilled,
a slow thumb-circle when I was unraveling,
a lingering hold when goodbye tasted too bitter.

Sometimes,
in the middle of a conversation,
she'd lift our joined hands and press her lips to mine

a kiss not meant for the mouth,
but for the soul.
As if to whisper:
"You're safe. You're loved. You're mine."

I didn't know hands could speak
until hers taught mine a new vocabulary.

She made me believe that love isn't always loud.
Sometimes, it's silent
like the hush between two hearts
that understand each other without explanation.

Even in our worst fights,
when distance grew and tempers flared,
her hand would find mine again
a truce offered not in words,
but in warmth.

I remember a day
we were walking past a gate,
and a dog barked, sharp and sudden.
I flinched.
She didn't.
She just tightened her grip around my fingers
and smiled.
Not a word spoken,
but everything said:
"I've got you."

And she did.
She always did.

In crowded places,
she'd find my hand without looking.
In dim theaters,

her fingers would curl into mine during the sad parts,
our pulses syncing like a shared heartbeat.

Sometimes I'd glance down at our hands and wonder,
How did something so simple become so sacred?

But the truth is,
her hand was never just a hand.
It was *home*.
It was safety.
It was understanding without question.
It was *her*.

And now
now that the space between our hands is permanent
I wonder how many people will live their whole lives
without knowing what it feels like
to be held that way.

Not just held,
but *understood*.

If soulmates exist,
maybe it's not about faces or voices
maybe it's the way two hands fit,
without effort,
without thought,
like the universe carved them from the same soft clay
just so they could find each other.

Even now,
when life gets heavy
and I feel myself slipping into the quiet again,
I remember the way her hand held mine
not as a lifeline,
but as a *promise*.

A promise that said:
You are not alone.
Not now.
Not ever.

Letter IV: The Way She Looked at Me

There was something about her eyes
not just their color,
not just their shape.
It was what lived behind them.
A language that didn't need words,
a softness that undressed my pride,
a gaze that made me feel like the only man in the world.

She didn't just *look* at me.
She *saw* me.
In ways I didn't even see myself.

There were times I was quiet
not out of peace,
but out of fear,
out of doubt,
out of exhaustion.
She would turn to me, tilt her head slightly,
and her eyes would narrow, not in suspicion
but in gentle concern.
As if saying, *"Talk to me. I'm here."*

When I spoke, she didn't glance, she *listened* with her eyes.
Those pupils dilated when I talked about something I loved,
as if her soul was leaning in to meet mine.
And when I stumbled over my words or fell short of being "enough,"
her eyes told me I already was.

She had this way of looking at me like I was art
like she was standing in front of a masterpiece that nobody else quite understood.
And while the world rushed by in gray,
her eyes painted me in color.

Like I was vibrant.
Like I was worthy.
Like I was someone to be *held,* not fixed.

I remember one evening, golden hour draped over her face,
and I caught her staring.
No smile. No words. Just her gaze.
And I asked her, "What?"
She said,
"Nothing. You just look like forever."

Her eyes were steady when the world wasn't.
On my worst days, they didn't flinch.
She looked at me with the same tenderness whether I was broken or brilliant.

And when I laughed
really laughed
her eyes sparkled,
not just from joy,
but from *pride.*
Like my happiness was her favorite story.

Even when she was mad,
even when she was tired,
even when she was lost in her own mind
she never looked at me with disgust.
She never looked through me.
She *always saw me.*

And in those moments,
I realized what made her different.
Most people look at you to judge,
to compare,
to measure.
But she

she looked at me like I was human,
and still worth loving.

And to be loved like that?
To be seen like that?

It changes you.

Even now, when she's not around,
when the noise of the world tries to drown me,
I remember those eyes
the way they held me without arms,
healed me without words,
and made me believe that maybejust maybe
I was someone worth looking at like that.

Letter V: The Way She Smiled When She Said My Name

There's something sacred
about hearing your name
in the voice of someone who *loves you.*

But when she said mine
it was different.
It wasn't just sound,
it was a song written just for me.

There was a softness in her tone
like she had rehearsed it a thousand times in her heart
before saying it aloud.

She would say my name as if it was her favorite secret,
a melody she only played for herself.
Slow sometimes,
like she didn't want to rush the syllables
as if each one held weight.
Other times, light and teasing,
like a spark dancing off her lips,
leaving a trail of laughter behind.

But every time…
every single time,
she smiled.

Even when she was tired,
even when life was too loud,
even when we hadn't spoken for hours
my name, from her mouth,
was a homecoming.

She would say it like she missed it.
Like saying it brought me closer, even if I was right there.

And that smile
that little lift at the corners of her lips,
sometimes hidden,
sometimes bursting
it wasn't just a smile.
It was a mirror.
It showed me what I looked like
through the eyes of someone who truly *saw* me.

When she said my name,
she wasn't calling me
she was *welcoming* me.

Like, "You're safe here."
Like, "I know you."
Like, "You matter."

And it didn't matter where we were
in a crowd,
in silence,
in chaos,
in distance
the way she said my name made everything else disappear.

There were moments I doubted myself.
Moments I felt like I was fading.
Moments the world felt heavy on my chest.

But then she'd say my name
just once
with that smile,
and suddenly,
I remembered who I was.

I think the world would be kinder
if everyone had someone who said their name
like she said mine.
If everyone knew what it felt like
to be loved without needing to earn it,
to be seen without needing to perform.

Because in that one act
in her smile,
in her voice,
in the simplicity of my name
she gave me a gift:
Belonging.

She made my name feel like a poem,
like a blessing,
like a promise.

And I carry it now,
even in her absence,
the echo of that smile stitched into each letter.

Letter VI: The Night Everything Felt Like Forever

There are nights that pass quietly,
without asking for attention
and then there are nights
that *stay.*

That night, with her,
didn't feel like a moment.
It felt like *eternity* had paused just for us.
Like time, for once, was kind enough to slow down.

The stars above didn't just shine
they watched.
The moon didn't just glow
it *listened.*

We weren't doing anything extravagant.
No grand stage.
No cinematic backdrop.
Just the two of us,
and a quiet world that had finally fallen asleep.

She leaned into me like she belonged there.
Like my shoulder had always been hers.
Our fingers, intertwined, fit without effort
as if they had been searching for each other since birth.

We talked about everything and nothing.
The kind of talk where silence didn't threaten
it comforted.
We laughed so easily,
like the sound had lived inside us all along,
waiting to be released by each other's presence.

She told me her favorite childhood memory.
I told her my biggest fear.
She didn't flinch.
She looked at me like I was *whole*,
not broken.

And then,
there was that moment.

The one I keep replaying.

Where she looked at me
really looked.
Her eyes shimmered, not with tears,
but with something deeper:
recognition.

Like she saw parts of me I didn't know how to show.
Like she had known me across lifetimes,
and finally found me again.

And she smiled,
and whispered my name,
and the way the night held it
was softer than any dream I'd ever known.

I didn't want to speak.
Didn't want to blink.
Didn't want to breathe too loud,
in case I'd break whatever spell we were wrapped in.

It was in that night
that I stopped searching for more.
Because for the first time
she was enough.

That night,
I didn't fall in love.

I *rested* in love.
Sank into it.
Let it carry me.

She made time irrelevant.
She made the stars jealous.
She made the darkness beautiful.

And when the world started to wake again,
and the first light crept in,
I held her hand tighter
because some part of me knew:

We would never get that exact moment again.
But we had it.
And that was enough
to last *forever*.

Letter VII: The Mornings with Her

She was different in the morning.
Not in the way people change after a long night's sleep,
but in the way the world feels softer when you finally feel safe.
She was softness.
She was stillness.
She was the reason I woke up smiling without meaning to.

Her hair was always a little wild,
falling in waves that the night forgot to tame.
She'd blink slowly at the sunlight slipping through the curtains,
eyes still heavy, but brighter than anything outside that window.
And then
that small smile,
the kind that only came in those first moments of waking,
like I was a dream she was relieved to still be in.

She never rushed the mornings.
She let them hold her gently.
She'd wrap herself in the blanket like a cocoon,
roll closer to me,
press her cold toes against my legs like it was a habit,
and mumble,
"Five more minutes,"
even though we had nowhere to be.

I would watch her breathe.
Slow.
Steady.
A rhythm I wanted to memorize.

She made those hours holy.
No alarms.
No chaos.

Just the smell of her skin,
and the silence filled with something sacred.

Sometimes, she'd hum quietly while brushing her hair.
Sometimes, she'd dance around the kitchen in socks,
burning the toast but laughing like it didn't matter.
And I'd sit there,
half-awake,
fully in love,
thinking
So this is what peace looks like.

She didn't know it,
but she taught me how beautiful ordinary could be.
Not with grand gestures,
but in the way she poured coffee with sleepy hands,
in the way she looked at the sky like it was new every day,
in the way she kissed my forehead like a promise before 9 a.m.

The world outside kept spinning,
but inside those mornings with her,
time curled up beside us.
It waited.
It watched.
It paused,
just long enough for me to fall deeper.

She turned mornings
those forgotten hours
into memories I still wake up missing.

If I could go back to one thing,
it wouldn't be the first kiss or the late-night talks
it would be the mornings.
The way she made them feel like a beginning.
The way she made me feel like home.

Letter VIII: Her Favorite Color Became Mine

It wasn't something she said loudly.
In fact, I don't remember her saying it at all at first
not in words.
She showed it,
the way people reveal what they love by how they treat it.

It was blue.
But not just any blue.
It was the kind of blue you find in between the sky and the sea.
The blue that changes with the light,
that hides a hundred different moods
some soft, some deep, some impossible to name.

She wore it in her clothes,
but only subtly
a scarf, a hair clip, sometimes the laces of her shoes.
She painted her nails that color once,
and I watched them move like waves when she spoke with her hands.

She once bought a mug, chipped and imperfect,
just because it was *that* shade.
She held it like it was made of memories,
like somehow it made her feel safe.

And slowly,
without meaning to
that color bled into me.

I began to notice it everywhere.
In the sky after rain.
In the way twilight stretched across empty streets.
In her favorite book cover,

in the plate she always reached for,
in the bedsheet that smelled like her every time I laid my head down.

It was just a color.
But it was also her.
It was how I remembered her in places she never stood.
It was how I felt close to her when we were apart.

When she talked about it really talked
she said it reminded her of peace,
of freedom,
of oceans and open skies and running barefoot through fields
with nothing to carry but hope.
She said it made her feel *light*,
like maybe, just maybe, the world wasn't as heavy as it seemed.

I never told her this,
but I started choosing it too
blue pens, blue shirts, blue lights on rainy evenings.
I began to crave that color in the same way I craved her.
It started to feel like breathing.
Like belonging.

Her favorite color became mine,
not because she asked me to love it,
but because everything she touched with it became softer
became *hers*.

And maybe that's what love is.
Letting someone's quiet joys soak into you,
until one day you look at a color
and don't just see blue
you see her eyes under sunlight,
her smile in the glow of a summer afternoon,
her laugh echoing across the horizon.

I see blue now,
and I see her.
And somehow, even after all this time,
it still feels like home.

Letter IX: When She Looked at Me Like I Was Enough

She didn't fix me.
She didn't try to.
She just sat across from me,
with her quiet eyes
and a smile
that didn't ask for more.

She listened to my silences
like they were full of meaning.
She never rushed me to speak.
She never asked me
to be louder
or bolder
or better.

She looked at me
like I was already all the things
I kept failing to become.

And maybe I said something stupid,
and maybe I looked away,
but her gaze stayed.

It stayed.

Like I didn't need fixing.
Like the cracks in me
were not just acceptable,
but beautiful.

She looked at me
like I had nothing to prove.
Like I didn't need to wear

my strength like armor.
Like the softness I hid
was the very thing
she cherished most.

There was something holy
in the way her eyes met mine.
Not the worship kind
but the honest kind.
The real kind.

She didn't ask for explanations
for my past,
or reasons for my scars.
She didn't flinch when I opened up.
She stayed.

She stayed
with those eyes
that made me believe
I was worth staying for.

I don't know if you've ever felt
what it's like
to finally be enough
for someone
just by breathing.

But I did.
That day.
With her.

And I carry that moment
like a secret blessing
the kind that saves you

when the rest of the world forgets
you're trying.

Because for once,
I wasn't trying.
I was just…
me.

And that was enough.

Letter X: The Smile I Wanted to Protect

It wasn't just pretty.
It was peace.

Her smile
it showed up like sunlight
through half-closed curtains,
gentle,
unexpected,
warm.

It wasn't the kind of smile
that asked for attention.
It was the kind
that asked you to stay.

I watched her laugh at the little things
the way her nose scrunched,
how her eyes disappeared,
how her whole face softened,
like even her sadness had let go
just for a moment.

And I knew.
I knew I'd do anything
to keep that smile safe.

From the world.
From pain.
From the weight
she carried in silence
when no one was watching.

I wanted to be
the reason it stayed.

The reason it came back
on hard days.

Not just when things were easy,
but when she wanted to fall apart
I wanted to be the arms
she could fall into
and still smile through the tears.

Her smile made everything else quiet.
It made time stop.
It made all the noise
in my own mind
slow down.

I didn't just love her.
I loved that part of her
she gave so freely,
even when she was hurting.

And maybe the world
wasn't always kind to her.
Maybe some days
she'd forget how to smile at all.

But I'd remember.
And I'd remind her.
Every time.
Over and over again

because her smile
was home.
And I'd protect it
like it was
the last light
in the dark.

PART III: LOSING HER

"Losing her didn't happen all at once.
It was a slow fading
a quiet shift from always to sometimes,
from good morning texts to unanswered nights.
And by the time I realized love was leaving,
she was already gone."

Echo I: The Day She Left

She didn't raise her voice.
She didn't cry.
She didn't even flinch.

She just looked at me
like she was already gone.
Like her heart had left
days before her feet did.

I asked her if this was it.
She nodded,
and in that small nod,
I felt something in me crack.

I didn't beg.
Not because I didn't want to,
but because I knew
she had already made peace with losing me.

She packed slowly,
like she had practiced this moment
in her head
a hundred times before.
Like she knew where everything was,
even the pieces of herself
she left in my room.

The hoodie she used to steal.
The toothbrush beside mine.
The half-read book on the shelf.
All untouched.
All left behind,
like they meant nothing now.

I asked if she’d be okay.
She said yes.
I didn’t ask if I would.

Because I knew
I wouldn’t.

The moment she walked out,
time slowed.
And every sound in the room
got louder.

The hum of the fan.
The tick of the clock.
My own breathing
sharp, uneven,
like my lungs forgot how to work
without her in the air.

I stood at the door
long after she was gone,
hoping maybe
this was all a mistake.

That she'd forgotten something.
That she'd turn around.
That she'd come running back.

But all she left
was her absence.
And it filled the whole room.

I kept replaying it
the way she didn’t cry,
the way she didn’t say “I love you,”
not even once.

She used to.
Every day.
Until she didn't.

I think the worst part
was not knowing
when she stopped trying.
When she stopped hoping.
When she stopped choosing me.

It's not the goodbye
that haunts me.
It's everything
she didn't say.

And I still wonder
did she feel it too?
That ache in the chest
when love begins to rot
from the inside out?

Maybe she just got tired.
Tired of waiting
for me to love her better.
Tired of giving
and never feeling full.

And now I sit with that
with the weight of what I didn't do,
with the silence she left behind,
with the version of me
that was never enough to make her stay.

Echo II: The Silence That Followed

After she left,
the world didn't stop.
But mine did.

The room stayed the same
but it felt colder.
Her laughter wasn't echoing off the walls anymore.
Her voice wasn't calling my name.

There was just… silence.

Not peaceful silence.
But the kind that feels like punishment.
The kind that screams
everything I did wrong.

I would wake up
and for a split second
forget she was gone.
I'd reach for her.
And my hand would land
on cold sheets
that forgot how to hold warmth.

I stopped playing music.
Because every song
sounded like her.

Even the ones
we never listened to.

I'd sit in the quiet
and stare at the door,
wondering if silence

could bring her back
the way noise pushed her away.

I stopped talking much.
Because what's the point
of saying things
when the one person
you want to hear them
isn't listening anymore?

The house started to rot
in stillness.
No more arguments.
No more soft conversations
at 2 a.m.
No more "I'm home."
No more "I missed you."

Just… nothing.

I talked to the walls sometimes.
Told them about my day.
As if they'd answer back
in her voice.

I missed her
in every sound I didn't hear.

No heels clicking on the floor.
No keys turning in the lock.
No whispered "goodnight."

Just the creak of loneliness
settling in.

My friends said I'd get used to it.
They said silence can be comforting.

But this silence?
This silence knew me too well.
It pointed at my chest
and asked,
"Why didn't you fight for her harder?"

And I had no answer.

So I just sat there.
With the weight of her absence
and the sound of everything
I'll never get back.

And the silence?
It stayed.
It never left.

Just like she didn't.

Echo III: I Miss Her in Crowds

It's strange,
how you can feel alone
surrounded by people.

Laughter everywhere.
Voices blending.
Lives moving.
But my heart… stuck.

I look at couples passing by
fingers intertwined,
eyes dancing with quiet love.
And I wonder
if she ever looks at someone
the way she used to look at me.

Sometimes, I hear a laugh
that sounds like hers.
I turn too fast,
hope blooming like a fool
only to face a stranger.

I hate crowds.
Not because of the noise.
But because in every face
I'm searching for one
I'll never find again.

I carry her with me
to cafes,
to train stations,
to late-night walks
I pretend I enjoy.

I talk less now.
Because she was the one
who made silence feel safe.
Now it's just a void
I try to fill
with small talk
and fake smiles.

They say move on.
They don't understand
I don't miss her in my room.
I miss her in the middle of chaos,
in the middle of everyone,
where she used to be my peace.

The world kept spinning,
but my favorite person
got off too early.

And every time I laugh now,
it feels borrowed.
Like I'm wearing joy
that doesn't fit me anymore.

She made crowds feel like home.
Now they feel like reminders.

Of what I had.
Of who I lost.
Of how even in a sea of people,
my eyes
still look for her.

Echo IV: Her Goodbye Broke Me Quietly

She didn't cry.
She didn't tremble.
She didn't even look back.

That's how I knew it was over.
Not because of what she said
but because of all the things she didn't.

She used to hold my hand
like it was home.
Now, she let go
like it was nothing.

No fight.
No last kiss.
Just a small sigh,
like love had finally
tired her out.

"I think we've reached the end,"
she whispered,
as if we were just some story
she didn't feel like finishing.

And I stood there,
full of everything
I should've said sooner,
everything I should've done differently,
everything I still felt
while she stood there
with nothing left.

Her eyes didn't shine anymore.
They used to light up
when they saw me.
Now they just passed through me,
like I was a stranger
in a place she used to love.

She didn't raise her voice.
She didn't make a scene.
She just left.
And somehow,
that quiet broke me more
than any scream ever could.

It was the silence
that hurt the most.
No slammed doors,
no "I hate you,"
no "don't go."

Just her back,
getting smaller with each step,
until there was nothing left
but the sound
of my own breath
trying to fill the space
she used to take up.

And even that
even that sounded wrong.

She left like a sunset.
Beautiful.
Slow.
Final.

And I?
I stood in the dark,
waiting for a dawn
that never came.

Her goodbye didn't echo.
It didn't scream.
It didn't bleed.

It whispered.
And I've been haunted
by that silence
ever since.

Echo V: The Things I Never Said

I had so much to tell her.
But I thought I had time.

I thought I'd say it next week,
next call,
next time we sat under stars,
her head on my shoulder,
when the world felt still.
But time didn't wait.
She left.
And the words stayed.

Now they echo in my chest
like unanswered prayers.

I should've told her
how my day got better
just seeing her name on my phone.
How her laugh
used to make my worst moments feel lighter.

I should've told her
that even when I was quiet,
I was still choosing her.
That the silence wasn't distance
it was fear.
Fear of being too much.
Fear of not being enough.

I should've told her
I noticed the little things:
how she tucked her hair behind her ear
when she was nervous,
how she traced circles on my palm

when she needed reassurance.
God, I miss that.

I should've told her
that her presence felt like peace
like home
like something I never wanted to lose.

But I stayed silent.
I thought love was obvious.
That she could see it
in the way I looked at her,
the way I remembered her coffee order,
the way I always walked on the side of traffic.

But maybe she needed words.
Maybe she needed to hear
that she was the best thing
that ever happened to me.

Maybe if I had told her,
she wouldn't have felt so alone
while standing beside me.

Now I sit here,
night after night,
writing paragraphs in my head
that she'll never read.
Practicing confessions
that will never be heard.

I still whisper her name sometimes
when no one's around,
just to remember
how it felt on my tongue.

I still tell her
I love her
just in places
she doesn't visit anymore.

She's gone.
And I'm full of everything
I never said.

If love could be measured
by the weight of unspoken words,
she'd know
I loved her
with everything I had,
and everything
I didn't know how to say.

Echo VI: About Her and the Distance

It didn't happen overnight.
She didn't just walk away.
She drifted.

Like a song fading at the end,
like smoke curling into nothing.
Each day,
a little further.
A little colder.

We used to talk for hours.
Then it became minutes.
Then replies.
Then read receipts.
Then… nothing.

And I told myself she was busy.
That she was tired.
That things would go back.
But they never did.

The space between us wasn't just physical.
It was emotional.
Spiritual.
Invisible but heavy.
A distance you couldn't map
but you could feel.
In your chest.
In the pit of your stomach.

She laughed less.
Smiled, but it didn't reach her eyes.
And I asked if she was okay.
She said she was "fine."

But “fine” was a lie
we both agreed to believe
because the truth was too heavy.

She started telling others things
she used to tell me.
Posting about moments
I wasn’t part of.
And every story I wasn’t in
felt like a goodbye
written in real time.

I tried to hold on.
Sent her songs.
Memes.
Memories.
But it was like trying to hold sand
the tighter I clenched,
the faster it slipped away.

She changed her hairstyle.
Started going places
we dreamed of going together
without me.
And I realized:
she was building a life
where I didn’t fit anymore.

The hardest part wasn’t her leaving.
It was knowing
she had already left
long before she said the words.
I just didn’t want to believe it.

About her and the distance?
It wasn’t just geography.

It was forgetting.
It was silence.
It was love thinning out
like breath in cold air
visible for a moment,
then gone.

I didn't lose her all at once.
I lost her
in pieces.
Slowly.
Painfully.
Until I was the only one
still holding on
to something
that no longer existed.

Echo VII: She Forgot Me Slowly

It wasn't sudden.
She didn't wake up one day and decide I no longer mattered.
No.
She forgot me the way stars disappear at dawn
slowly,
quietly,
without anyone noticing.

At first, it was the little things.
She stopped asking if I'd eaten.
Stopped sending those goodnight texts
that once made my whole day feel worth it.
Stopped caring about my silence
because hers was louder.

I remember telling her a story once
a memory of us,
something beautiful
and she smiled like a stranger,
like she was hearing it for the first time.
Like I was someone else
talking about a different girl.

That broke me.

She used to remember everything
how I took my coffee,
the scar on my hand,
my favorite song when I was sad.
Now, she didn't even flinch
when I mentioned things we once swore we'd never forget.

I watched her memory of me dissolve
like ink in water

there,
then gone.
No fight.
No fire.
Just fading.

And the cruelest part?
I remembered everything.
Her laugh.
The way she hummed songs under her breath.
How she looked when she said my name
like it meant something.

I held on to all of it.
While she…
she let go.

She deleted pictures slowly
first from stories,
then from posts,
then from her phone.
She removed me like dust
from a shelf she didn't need anymore.
Gently.
Almost respectfully.

But it still hurt.
God, it hurt.

She started saying "I" instead of "we."
She stopped liking my messages.
Stopped viewing my stories.
Like she was training herself
to live without me.
And it worked.

She forgot the way I looked at her
when she wasn't watching.
The way I prayed for her
when she couldn't sleep.
The way I loved her
fully,
desperately,
gently.

I became a ghost in her past
a closed tab in her browser,
a name that stopped ringing any bells.

And maybe one day she'll hear a song
or visit a place
and something will ache for a second
a flicker,
a feeling
she won't quite place.
That'll be me.
That'll be what's left of us.
Just a whisper of a love
she slowly forgot
while I remembered too much.

Echo VIII: When Love Wasn't Enough

I loved her.
God knows I did.

I loved her in ways words will never be able to explain.
I loved her quietly when she was tired,
loudly when she laughed,
completely when she didn't love herself.
I loved her through every storm,
through every silence,
through every version of hereven the one that didn't love me back.

But sometimes…
love is not enough.

We grow up being told love conquers all,
that if you love hard enough,
fight strong enough,
hold on long enough
everything will fall into place.
But no one tells you
that sometimes, even the deepest love
can't make someone stay.

She didn't leave because I didn't love her.
She left because love wasn't fixing the cracks.
Because smiles became forced.
Because even while we held hands,
it felt like we were slipping.

I remember sitting next to her,
our shoulders touching,
but our hearts miles apart.
She smiled at her phone

and I smiled at her
but neither of us smiled for real.

It's a strange kind of tragedy
when love still exists
but can't carry the weight anymore.
We stopped laughing like we used to.
Stopped talking about tomorrow.
Every 'I love you' started sounding like an apology.

And I kept thinking
if I just try harder,
if I just love her a little more,
maybe things will go back.
Maybe she'll look at me
like I'm still her home.

But love isn't a glue.
It's a fire
and even fire dies when the air runs out.

I watched us fall apart in slow motion.
No shouting, no final fight, no slamming doors.
Just long silences,
short replies,
and eyes that once saw forever now avoiding mine.

And the worst part?

We still loved each other.
But it wasn't enough to stay.
It wasn't enough to heal.

She needed peace.
I needed her.
And sometimes those two things
just don't live in the same place.

So she left
with my heart in her hands,
and tears she didn't show me.
She said goodbye like it was mercy,
like letting go was saving both of us
from becoming more broken than we already were.

And I…
I let her go
because loving her meant wanting her happy
even if it wasn't with me.

So now I carry a love
with nowhere to go
a house with no lights,
a heart with no name to beat for.

I loved her.
And that will always be true.
But love,
as much as we wish it could
isn't always enough.

Echo IX: I Waited, She Didn't Come Back

I waited.

Every day.

At first, I waited with hope.
The kind that clings to the edge of reason.
The kind that makes you check your phone at 3AM
just in case she remembered
what you used to mean to each other.

I waited in silence,
because texting her felt like trespassing
on a heart that no longer belonged to me.
I thought maybe,
just maybe,
she'd walk through the same old memories
and realize how warm they still were.

But days turned into weeks,
and all I got was silence.
Not the peaceful kind
but the kind that screams in your chest,
echoing louder the more you try to ignore it.

I told myself stories to survive.
"She's just figuring things out."
"She misses me too, she just doesn't know how to say it."
"She'll come back when she's ready."

But she didn't.
And eventually,
those stories started sounding more like lies
I told to keep from falling apart.

I waited at the café we used to sit in
ordered her favorite drink,
even though I hated the taste.
I kept her number pinned on top of my chats,
like it mattered,
like she'd one day text "I miss you,"
and everything would go back.

I waited on her birthday.
Didn't text.
Didn't call.
But I stared at her name
for an hour
before deleting and rewriting the message
a dozen times
until it was just me,
alone,
with words that would never be sent.

I waited for the apology
that never came.
For the knock on the door
that never echoed.
For the closure
that love stories never really give you.

And slowly
painfully
I realized that I wasn't waiting for her.
I was waiting for who she *used* to be.
And that person?
She was gone long before she ever left.

They say if you love someone, let them go.
But they never say
what to do when they don't come back.

They don't tell you
that some nights will feel like dying
and some mornings like survival.
That healing isn't loud
it's quiet and cruel
and comes in pieces
you find in your old shirts,
her old songs,
and the way your bed still feels too big.

I waited,
until waiting started to hurt more than the goodbye.
Until hope became heavy.
Until my heart whispered,
"She's not coming back."

And that's when I knew
I wasn't healing because I was still holding the door open.
So I locked it.
Quietly.
Without anger.
Without blame.

Just with the acceptance
that sometimes the person you want the most
is the one you have to let go of
to find yourself again.

She didn't come back.

But maybe…
just maybe…

someday,
I will.

Echo X: I Still Write Her Name Sometimes

I still write her name sometimes.

Not on purpose.
Not because I expect her to come back.
It's more like muscle memory
the way your hand knows the motion
before your heart knows the reason.

It slips out in margins,
in empty corners of notebooks,
between the lines of poems I don't finish.
I'll be jotting down thoughts
and suddenly realize
that somewhere,
without even noticing,
I've written her name.

Just her name.

As if it still means something.

And I guess, in a way, it does.

Not in the way it used to.
Not in the "she's mine" kind of way.
But in the "she once was" kind of way.
The kind that doesn't demand a future
but still honors the past.

I still write her name when the world is quiet.
When the weight of memory feels softer than usual.
When I remember how her laughter
used to live in the spaces I now fill with silence.

Sometimes, I trace the letters slowly,
like each one holds a different version of her
the girl she was when she loved me,
the girl she became when she left,
and the stranger she is now.

People think forgetting is some kind of progress.
But I don't think I'll ever forget her.
Not completely.
You don't forget the ones
who taught you how to fall apart beautifully.

I still write her name in my mind
when I hear that one song,
or pass by that place,
or catch a scent that carries me back
to a version of me
that existed only in her presence.

And no
it doesn't hurt like it used to.
It doesn't feel like drowning anymore.
Now it feels more like
standing beside a grave
you've visited too many times
you no longer cry,
you just stay a little while
and whisper,
"Thank you, for what you were."

I still write her name sometimes
because I'm not trying to erase her.

She was part of my story.
A chapter I once read a thousand times,
underlined, highlighted,

dog-eared every page.
And even though I've moved on to new chapters,
I still flip back sometimes,
just to feel how it used to feel.

Not to stay.
Just to remember.

So if you ever find her name scribbled in the corner of my journal,
don't ask me why.

Some names
don't fade.
They just stop echoing.

And if someday she ever reads this,
I hope she knows
even though I no longer chase her,
no longer wait for her,
no longer break for her…

I still write her name sometimes.
Because love like that
doesn't vanish.

It simply
learns
to live
quietly.

PART IV: LIVING WITHOUT HER

"Healing isn't forgetting.
It's learning to remember without breaking.
To carry the love without the ache.
She's not mine anymore
but some nights, I still thank the stars that she once was."

Reflection I: If She's Reading This...

If she's reading this,
I want her to know I still remember her laugh
not the one everyone saw,
but the one that slipped out when she forgot the world.

I still remember how she looked
when she was trying not to cry
but smiled anyway
like she didn't want me to worry.

If she's reading this,
tell her I never stopped looking at the moon
hoping it reaches her too.
I hope she still sings in the shower
and dances in front of the mirror
when no one's watching.
I hope someone loves her like I tried to.

If she's reading this,
I want her to know
I never wanted to be her past.
I wanted to grow old with her.
I wanted forever.

But life had other plans.

If she's reading this,
tell her I still whisper her name
in rooms she used to light up.
Tell her the silence hasn't left.
Tell her I keep writing,
because forgetting her feels like betrayal.

If she's reading this…
I'm sorry.
For everything I said.
And for everything I never said.
If she's reading this,
I hope she knows
I loved her with everything I had,
and maybe that wasn't enough,
but it was real.

If she's reading this...
I hope she smiles.
Even if it's not because of me.

Reflection II: About Her and the Ghost She Left

She left.
But not all of her.

There are parts of her
still sitting on the side of my bed
where she used to laugh
at things only I could say.

I can still see her shadow
in the corner of every quiet room.
She doesn't knock anymore,
but she enters
with every song,
every scent,
every name that even sounds like hers.

I sleep alone now,
but the ghost she left sleeps beside me.
And sometimes,
she pulls me into dreams
so vivid I wake up
trying to hold onto someone
who's been gone for years.

The ghost of her doesn't scream.
She whispers.
And her whispers hurt more.

She shows up in conversations
I never start,
but somehow always finish with her name.
My friends don't ask about her anymore

but they still see it in my eyes
when I drift off mid-sentence.

It's funny
how a body can leave
but a presence remains.
How someone can say goodbye
and still be here
in the way I flinch
at her favorite songs,
or look twice
at girls who wear their hair like hers.

I keep saying I'm healing.
But the ghost she left
still holds the part of me
that believed in forever.

I dated again.
Smiled again.
Tried again.
But no one fits like her silence does.
No one feels like her absence.

She left me
with every version of herself
she shared.
And I carry them
in the ache behind my smile,
in the weight of empty spaces,
in the songs I skip,
in the ones I still play on repeat.

This chapter isn't about who she was.
It's about the ghost she became
and how she still walks through me

like a wind I can't stop,
but always feel.

Reflection III: Every Girl After Her

Every girl after her
has walked into a losing game.

They didn't know
they were stepping into a space
already occupied
by someone who left,
but never really left.

I smiled at them,
but it never reached the part of me
she broke.

I listened
but I was always waiting to hear *her* voice
in someone else's mouth.
The way she used to say my name
like it meant something.

Every girl after her
was measured against memories
they never made,
compared to a ghost
they never saw.

I tried.
God, I tried.
To let someone else touch me
without feeling like I was cheating
on the pain she left behind.

But no matter how soft their hands,
no one could trace the places
she kissed and made sacred.

I laughed again
but it felt like betrayal.
Like joy was something
I wasn't allowed to keep
if she wasn't the reason.

They all asked me,
"Are you still in love with her?"
And I never had the courage to lie.

Because yes
every girl after her
was a page in a book
I couldn't finish
because I kept re-reading
the chapter she was in.

And maybe that's my fault
loving someone so deeply
that I turned everyone else
into her shadow.

But the truth is,
when you lose someone like her,
you don't move on.
You just keep walking
with her ghost
a step behind you.

Every girl after her
deserved better
than a heart still bleeding
from a goodbye
that never healed.

But I had nothing left to give.
Because she didn't just take my love
she took the version of me
who knew how to love again.

Reflection IV: When I Saw Her Again

When I saw her again,
the world didn't stop
but my heart did.

She looked different.
Not in the way people change,
but in the way time
softens memories
and hardens reality.

Her smile didn't have
my name behind it anymore.

She was laughing,
but not with me.
Happy,
but not because of me.
Alive,
in a life I no longer fit in.

And in that moment,
I realized something cruel
we don't always lose people
when they leave.
Sometimes,
we lose them
when they come back
and don't feel like home anymore.

I watched her like
you watch a sunset you used to chase
close enough to see,
too far to hold.

She didn't see me.
Or maybe she did,
and just looked through me
like I was someone she once knew
in a different lifetime.

And maybe I was.

Because the version of me
that loved her
died the day she left
and the version of her I carried
never really existed
outside my memory.

I thought I'd say something.
Something poetic.
Something final.
But all I could do
was breathe in her silence
and exhale the years
I spent writing her name
into every lonely night.

When I saw her again,
I didn't feel anger.
I didn't feel closure.
I just felt the quiet ache
of realizing
she had become a story
I kept telling
long after the ending.

And maybe that's what heartbreak really is
not the moment they leave,
but the moment they return

and you finally understand
they were never coming back
the way you needed them to.

Reflection V: The Dreams Where She Returns

She comes back to me in dreams.
Not like the girl who left
but like the girl I still love.

No baggage. No goodbyes.
Just her smile,
soft and whole,
like nothing ever broke us.

In those dreams,
we sit on rooftops,
talk about forever
like it still belongs to us.
She reaches for my hand,
and I don't flinch
because in dreams,
we're still safe.

She laughs at my jokes.
Wipes away my worries.
Tells me she missed me.
Tells me she never meant to go.
And I believe her,
every time.

But I always wake up
to an empty room
and a heart that remembers
what my mind tries to forget.

I don't know if it's comfort
or cruelty

that she still visits me there
in sleep,
where I can't stop her,
where I can't tell if it's love
or just my loneliness
wearing her face.

Sometimes,
I try to go back to sleep
just to find her again.
And sometimes,
I stay awake
because I know
she only lives
in the places I can't keep her.

They say dreams are wishes.
But I think mine are memories
too stubborn to die.

And maybe that's the saddest part
not that she left,
but that even in my dreams,
she always leaves again.

Reflection VI: Healing Is Remembering Without Crying

There was a time when just her name
was enough to wreck me.

A song,
a scent,
an old photo
it would send me spiraling.
Back to her.
Back to us.
Back to everything that broke.

But now…
I remember her
and I don't fall apart.

I remember her laugh,
and it makes me smile
before it makes me sad.
I remember her eyes,
and they don't haunt me
they just remind me
that once, I was seen.

I used to think healing meant forgetting.
Erasing every trace of her.
Burning the letters,
deleting the photos,
pretending we never happened.

But healing
isn't pretending.

It's remembering
without bleeding.

It's knowing she was real
and that what we had
was beautiful,
even if it wasn't forever.

It's finally understanding
that not everyone who comes
is meant to stay,
but that doesn't make their love
any less true.

I still miss her
but the missing feels different now.
Softer. Quieter.
Like a wound
that's finally closed,
but left a mark
where it mattered.

I no longer ache to bring her back.
I just carry her memory
with gentleness.

Because healing
isn't about forgetting her.
It's about remembering
and still being able
to breathe.

Reflection VII: She Was a Lesson, Not a Loss

She wasn't mine forever.
But she was mine for a while.
And in that while,
she changed me.

I could sit here
and count all the ways she hurt me,
but I won't.
Because even in the hurting,
there was something sacred.

She taught me how deep love could go
how loud silence could feel
and how sometimes,
the right person comes
at the wrong time
just to teach you
who you are without them.

She was a storm
I never wanted to end.
And when it passed,
I realized the flood
had carved something permanent
in me.

She made me softer.
More patient.
More human.

She showed me that love
isn't always about holding on

sometimes it's learning
how to let go
without hating the goodbye.

She wasn't a mistake.
She was a mirror.

She showed me what I needed,
what I lacked,
and what I still had to become.

And for that
for all of it
I don't call her a loss anymore.

She was a chapter,
not the whole story.
She was the lesson,
not the end.

And though she's gone,
what she left behind in me
still blooms.

Reflection VIII: I Hope She's Loved Now

I don't know where she is.
I don't know who holds her hand now,
or who gets to hear her laugh
in the mornings.

But I hope he listens.
Really listens.
The way I sometimes didn't.
I hope he knows
that her silence doesn't mean she's okay,
it means she's holding back tears.

I hope he tells her
how beautiful she is
when she doesn't feel it.
And I hope he never makes her beg
for the bare minimum.

I hope he asks about her favorite songs,
and knows why she skips the sad ones.
I hope he kisses her forehead,
not just her lips.
And when she cries
God, I hope he stays.

I used to think
no one could love her like I did.
But maybe someone will love her better.
Gentler.
Wiser.

And though the thought
cuts through my ribs
like it always did
I still hope she's loved now.
Fully.
Finally.
The way I once tried to.
The way she always deserved.

Reflection IX: What I'd Say If I Could

If I could speak to her now,
just once,
without the weight of the past between us,
I'd try to keep it simple.

I wouldn't beg her to come back.
I wouldn't ask her to miss me.
I'd just say:

"Hey.
Thank you.
For loving me when you did.
For the warmth,
the late-night laughs,
the way your name felt like home
on my tongue."

I'd tell her that I still carry her
not out of pain anymore,
but out of respect.
Because even though we ended,
she mattered.

I'd say I'm sorry.
For the days I didn't show up fully.
For the times I thought loving her
was enough
without showing it properly.

I'd tell her I still write about her sometimes,
in poems that no one reads
and dreams I don't always share.

I'd tell her I hope she found peace,
not just happiness
because peace stays
even when the music stops.

And if she smiled,
even a little,
I'd finally exhale
the goodbye I never got to say.

That's what I'd say.
If I could.

Reflection X: About Her, Always.

They'll ask me about her.

And I'll pause
not because I've forgotten,
but because some names deserve silence
before they are spoken.

I'll say,
"She was a quiet kind of magic.
The kind you don't notice right away
until it's already changed you."

They'll wonder if I still love her.
And I'll smile, not with lips,
but with the ache in my chest.

I'll say,
"I don't know what to call it now
but love like that doesn't vanish.
It just finds quieter ways to stay."

They'll ask why we ended.
And I'll say,
"Sometimes even the stars fall out of orbit.
Even the right hearts meet at the wrong time."

They'll ask if I ever moved on.
And I'll say,
"I kept walking, yes.
But there are parts of me
still sitting beside her,
in conversations we never finished."

They'll ask if I hate her.

And I'll say,
"No.
I loved her too deeply
to ever turn that into hate.
She's the chapter I never skip,
no matter how many times I reread my story."

They'll ask what she meant to me.
And I'll say,
"She taught me how love feels.
How it breaks.
How it stays even after it's gone."

And maybe, years from now,
when she hears my name
I hope she pauses too.
Not in pain, but in peace.
Because what we had was real.
And no ending can take that away.

This book may close here.
But between every word,
every breath,
every ache
it was always about her.

Always.

www.ingramcontent.com/pod-product-compliance
Ingram Content Group UK Ltd.
Pitfield, Milton Keynes, MK11 3LW, UK
UKHW041346190726
13845UKWH00026B/456

9 789334 374551